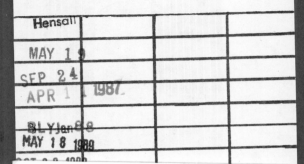

British Columbia

Pacific Dogwood, the floral
emblem of British Columbia,
in Vancouver's Stanley Park.

MAR 2 6 1981

63910

At the top of the Roger's Pass in the Selkirk Range.

British Columbia

This book is dedicated to Art and Edith Brooks
who brought me into this world

Copyright © 1980 by Bill Brooks
All rights reserved
ISBN 0-88882-050-x

Photographs and text: Bill Brooks

Design: René Demers
Craib Demers Associates Limited

Editor: John Robert Colombo

Publisher: Anthony Hawke

Printer: The Hunter Rose Company Ltd.

Typesetting: Kerr Graphics Limited

Hounslow Press
A Division of Anthony R. Hawke Limited
124 Parkview Avenue
Willowdale, Ontario, Canada M2N 3Y5

Printed in Canada

The Seabus takes another
load of commuters across
Vancouver's Burrard Inlet.

British Columbia

Paradise on the Pacific

British Columbia is almost too good to be true. It has just about everything: the big-city atmosphere of Vancouver, the wild west of Kamloops and Williams Lake, or the gentility of Victoria. There are places to suit every taste.

Are you the landless offspring of poor parents, eager to make your mark in life? Then go north to the frontier, where a person is judged by what he can do in a day, not by what his grandfather did in days gone by. The entire northern half of the province is a vast wilderness, overflowing with opportunity for the type of person who is willing to put his back to the wheel.

But wait a minute . . . perhaps you enjoy the big-city life, the art galleries, the latest fashions, the theatre, first-run movies, fine restaurants, and the world of business. Then Vancouver is for you. The San Francisco of the North, Vancouver is one of the most civilized cities in the world.

Tired of urban problems and the nine-to-five routine? Then take your boat up a trackless coast that is still as remote and as wild as it was in the day when the Nootka hunted the great whale in their sea-going canoes. If you have only your two feet to transport you, then go to the high country and take a walk on a mountain trail through the territory of the grizzly bear and the mountain goat. You will experience the solitude and oneness with self that can only be gained on a mountaintop.

If you are looking for a place to retire, then Victoria or the Gulf Islands, with their laid-back atmosphere and mild winters, are easy on bones that are starting to feel the weight of years gone by.

Most people, and certainly most British Columbians, do not fit into any one convenient slot. In my own case, while I might think the mountains are the greatest of God's creations, and I might ache for them when forced to be away, I still need to get high on the odd shot of big-city sophistication to keep my

life on an even keel. No matter how long I may have spent in my favourite place, I am always ready for a change of scene.

Change is the thing that keeps the juices flowing. The change of scene allows us to moderate our lifestyle and therefore our thinking processes. We do not become slaves to one particular set of circumstances. We can "get away," "take a break," and return refreshed. The more accessible the other life is, the better it is for us.

In British Columbia, the city, the small town, the wilderness, and the frontier are all in close proximity. A

person of modest means can work at a job all day yet spend his evenings and weekends attending symphony concerts, taking in gallery openings, walking on mountain tops, or sailing his boat among misty islands.

The experience of having all things at your doorstep creates a secure, happy people who are able to assign realistic values to the multitude of different activities that make up their lives. If there is one thing that characterizes British Columbians, it is their ability to get the tough job done, without losing sight of the fact that a life without fun and variety is no life at all.

In British Columbia you can, indeed, have your cake and eat it too.

Vancouver

Splendour Undiminished

Situated where the Fraser River empties into the Pacific, with the Coast Mountains as a backdrop, Vancouver has the most beautiful setting of any city in the world. The lights of the city centre glow golden on spring evenings, while sailing vessels ride at their moorings in False Creek and skiers take their runs on the floodlit slopes of Grouse Mountain beyond.

Only ten minutes from downtown by bus, Third Beach in Stanley Park is close enough for a lunch-time swim ... a swim that, on a warm sunny summer day, could easily stretch through the afternoon up to the dinner hour.

With the Bloedel Conservatory in Queen Elizabeth Park as a backdrop, an early-riser refreshes her mind and body with Tai Ch'i, ancient Chinese exercises.

Late afternoon finds many Vancouverites taking their leisure on the ski runs atop Grouse Mountain. The elevation provides a view of the office tower they so unabashedly excused themselves from only a short time before.

One of Vancouver's early characters was a saloon-keeper named Gassy Jack, who called the area around his pub Gastown. Ever-proud of their colourful roots, Vancouverites have erected a statue to Gassy Jack and call the area Gastown, in his honour.

A bit of West Coast whimsy, this clock, powered by steam from a duct under Water Street, toots the hours and never fails to amuse tourists and townee alike.

more expensive attraction
ross the street from the
am clock, are the windows
exclusive shops displaying
e latest in fashions.

A gentle rain blowing in off
the Pacific reflects the lights
of Vancouver's Chinatown
in the pavement of Pender
Street and sends pedestrians
scurrying for cover.

The Coast

Islands and Inlets

From the Queen Charlotte Islands in the north to the Strait of Juan de Fuca in the south, British Columbia's Pacific coast is a maze of islands, inlets, straits, sounds, bays, and channels. The Coast Range rises majestically out of the water's edge, and great fingers of the sea contained in submerged valleys poke their way inland among the peaks. A few brave men in small boats cruise this largely uninhabited labyrinth in search of fish.

Life along British Columbia's coast is dominated by the arrival and departure of the ferry. For many remote coastal villages and all of the islands, the ferry is the only connection with the outside world. Outsiders will fuss and fume over the time wasted on docks or decks. Locals, whether waiting on the deck of the *Queen of Prince Rupert* in the Inside Passage or waiting for a smaller ferry to dock at one of the Gulf Islands, use the enforced inactivity as an opportunity to relax and catch up on the local gossip.

Treasures washed up on the
beach are displayed by
the owner of this cabin on
Quadra Island.

What better way to experience
the rugged majesty of the
coast than to go for an evening stroll along the beach in
Pacific Rim National Park?

Another species of beach-
comber, the great blue heron
has a practical bent, for he
will swallow his prize in one
quick gulp.

Flung by the forces of
yesterday's storm, weathered
skeletons of driftwood rest
helter-skelter behind the rock
beach of Vancouver Island's
aptly named Wreck Bay.

As the evening sun sinks into the Pacific, a solitary figure wades shoeless into the surf and stares absent-mindedly as gentle waves wash away the cares of the day.

and from the beach on the
een Charlotte Islands
nds a moss-draped forest of
nt trees, growing so tall
d thick that the sun cannot
ch the forest floor.

A great tree rests on the forest
floor in Cathedral Grove
near Port Alberni. As it decays
it provides the space and the
sustenance for the new tree
that sprouts from its crum-
bling body.

In coastal areas, logs are brought to the sea where they are tied together into booms to be towed to the mill. Drawing on skills acquired through years of experience, an old hand walks a turning, bobbing log in the booming grounds at Kelsey Bay.

Rippling muscles and skills learned in the woods are put to good use winning cash prizes in the logging contests that are held around the province.

The dark clouds of a passing
Pacific storm and the fresh
bright green of a recently wet
forest are reflected in the
waters of Alice Lake on Vancouver Island.

On the Sunshine Coast at Gibsons, a forest of schooner masts reaches up to the peaks of the Coast Range.

Northern sea lions frolic in
the surf or climb up on small
islands along the entire coast.

Wet westerly winds, blowing
in off the Pacific, dump
record snowfalls, as they rise
up the slopes of the Coast
Range, seen here at Pember-
ton Meadows.

Terminus of the Canadian National railway, end of the Yellowhead Highway, and jumping-off point for Alaska and the interior, Prince Rupert is the northern anchor of British Columbia's Pacific shore.

The area is so popular with
fishermen that their boats are
moored three or four abreast
in Prince Rupert's harbour.

native carver practises the
rt of his ancestors in creating
new the totem poles that
sed to tower over shorelines
f the ancient villages.

This totem pole stares out
over 'Ksan, an authentic
reconstruction of an ancient
Kitksan Indian village on
the banks of the Skeena River
near Hazelton.

On the Bulkley River, where it passes through the reservation at Moricetown, a young Indian brave *(right)* inches towards the white water hoping to catch a leaping salmon *(left)*.

The North

The Wild Frontier

The vast wilderness of rock and bush making up the northern half of the province is penetrated by only two main roads, the Cassiar Road in the west and the Alcan Highway in the east.

Resources development on these two roads requires a continuous supply of men and machinery. Centres like Fort St. John on the Alcan have mushroomed overnight to meet this need. Here is the last outpost of civilization on the edge of the wilderness. Travellers heading out of town up the Alcan are happy to leave the pizza parlours behind. On the return trip south, after twelve-hour workdays and evenings talking to trees, attitudes have changed, and approaching this bit of civilization is like approaching an oasis in the desert, a little bit of heaven on earth.

n the Cassiar Road the dust
everywhere. Drivers turn on
adlights in the middle of
e day to see and be seen in
e fog-like dust cloud created
y two vehicles passing.

If you can stand the dust, you
can penetrate a beautiful wild
country seen by only a few
white men. Here ice floes, sun
cut from the front of the
magnificent Bear Glacier,
bump up against the embank-
ments of the Cassiar Road.

The grasses that grow in the
clearings created by logging
operations in the north
provide a succulent meal for
the Mule Deer.

A frequent visitor to the
cookhouses and garbage pails
of the logging camps, this
black bear contents himself
with a more natural delicacy
of fresh berries.

The Peace River area is changing, and such wilderness scenes as this canoe on Moberly Lake are giving way to more pastoral scenes, like these farmer's fields bordering the Peace River near Attachie.

Victoria

Garden City

Perched above the Pacific on the southwestern-most tip of the Province, Victoria enjoys mild winters and pleasant cool summers. This makes it a popular retirement community for Western Canadians tired of the extremes of climate common in interior regions. We are reminded, by the glowing outline of the Legislative Buildings overlooking the Inner Harbour, that Victoria is also the seat of government and the administrative centre for a vast province.

Victoria is ever proud of its
British heritage, although
those who take the traditional
afternoon tea at the Empress
Hotel are likely to be tourists from the United States,
Germany, and Japan.

Victoria probably has more
china shops per capita than
any city in Canada. Here a
couple of china junkies get
their fix in a shop on Fort
Street.

Continuing the British
theme, double-decker London
buses lie in wait outside
the Empress Hotel, ready to
whisk the tourist on a whirl-
wind tour of the local sights.

This fruit-seller in period
costume has set up shop in
Bastion Square, a refurbished
complex of restaurants,
boutiques, and offices in the
old section of the city.

The Interior

Between the Mountains

The interior of British Columbia is a vast area of low mountains, lakes, valleys, and plateau. The winds that blow across this area have been stripped of most of their moisture by the Coast Range to the west, so the area is mostly dry cattle country. Valleys, however, have lakes for irrigation, so the winds again drop moisture on the eastern edge of the area, as they rise up the western slopes of the Cariboo, Columbia, and Rocky Mountains. Here fishermen get an early-morning start on a lake in the Cariboo district.

Cattle graze in the shadow of the Cariboo Mountains near McBride.

Cattle country would not
be cattle country without
cowboys. Every small town
has a rodeo, and amateur
and professional alike come
to compete, as they do here,
in the pony-wagon race.

The Gold Rush to the Cariboo in the 1860s and the need for law and order led to the creation of the Province of British Columbia. Here, at Barkerville Provincial Historic Park, modern gold-rushers can, for a modest sum, try their hand at panning for the gold left behind by those early miners.

Barkerville grew up around
the gold claims on Williams
Creek. On its main street,
miners could avail themselves
of the services of both
the church and the saloon.

The wilderness has many kinds of beauty. The falling waters of Helmcken Falls, which drop 137 metres in Wells Gray Provincial Park, are not at all like the still waters of Bowron Lake, in Bowron Lake Provincial Park.

The Fraser River winds across the dry interior of the province. It is too fast and wild to float a boat for long, as many early travellers found to their dismay. The first major highway in the province, a wagon road to the Cariboo goldfields,. followed the Fraser's steep banks, here at a point near Lillooet.

Although rarely seen, cougars still roam the dry ranch country of the interior.

A pair of horses find the only shade in a near desert at Walhachin. At one time this valley was a paradise filled with fruit trees. However, the hard-working farmers served in World War I. The irrigation flumes fell into disrepair, the fruit trees wilted and died, and the few men who returned after the War found their dreams had turned to dust.

Rivers running off the neighbouring mountain ranges fill these dry valleys with water. It is hard to believe, when you are standing on the dock at Osoyoos or water-skiing on Christina Lake, that these valleys have one of the lowest rainfalls in Canada.

Fort Steele was named after Sam Steele, the North West Mounted Police Superintendent who, in 1887, averted an Indian uprising in East Kootenay. The town went into decline when it was bypassed by the railway. Today the old buildings have been restored, and the provincial government runs it as an historic park.

As civilization advances, the few remaining grizzly bears in the province are retreating to safety in the least-accessible of wildernesses. The road-bound tourist, however, can still come face-to-face with a grizzly at the Penticton Game Farm.

Perched on the banks of the
Columbia River at the bottom
of Lower Arrow Lake,
Castlegar is just downstream
from the Hugh Keenleyside
Dam.

There was a mining boom in the West Kootenay region in the 1890s; but, as with all mines, the ore eventually ran out. Today the area is haunted by the remains of ghost-like mine workings, such as these old headframes at Zincton.

Another relic of the mining days is this sternwheeler, the *S.S. Moyie*, now used as a museum at Kaslo. A fleet of these craft once cruised Kootenay Lake, carrying supplies and passengers for the mines. The *Moyie*, the last of the species, was put into drydock in 1957.

Upper Arrow Lake was
created and is controlled by
the huge dam at Castlegar.
Boaters and walkers along the
shoreline near Galena must
be on the lookout for sudden
changes in the lake level.

Slowly moving reflections of surrounding trees lull this fisherman on Box Lake into a semi-hypnotic state of perfect bliss. At a time like this, who cares who catches fish?

High Country

Where the Wind Blows Lonely

This is a fragile land, largely untouched by man. Parts are locked under perpetual ice and snow; most is uncut by roads. The mountains have a strange effect on the traveller. It may be the beauty, the solitude, or the feeling of being at peace with oneself that one experiences on a mountaintop. Whatever it is, the spell has me in its grip. No matter how far I may be from my beloved mountains, I will always be there, at the summit, in my mind.

The meadows on Mount Revelstoke are in full bloom in August. Here the warming rays of the morning sun reflect, from a multi-coloured carpet of wildflowers, an exquisite tapestry showing every colour of the rainbow.

High up in the Pine Pass through the Rocky Mountains, a bald eagle soars on updrafts created by the surrounding cliffs.

The author's wife walks at eagle-level on the Stanley Glacier Trail in Kootenay National Park.

These mountains teem with wildlife. Here a bighorn ram rejoins the herd just prior to the fall rut.

This solitary bull elk, feeding at a mountainside meadow, will soon be putting his magnificent antlers to good use in the fall competition for the female.

The hoary marmot builds its burrow under a rock in the high country above the tree line. Its shrill, whistle-like call often startles travellers walking through the high passes.

The white-tailed ptarmigan shares the same high range as the hoary marmot. This specimen is changing its brown summer coat over to winter white.

The Asulkan Pass in Glacier
National Park is still in the
grip of a glacier, visible on
the right and top centre. This
is wild country. Only a few
hardy lichens and mosses
grow here, and even moun-
tain goats seek out lower
elevations. As he picks his
way along the ridges and over
the rocks, thrown helter-
skelter by the advancing
glacier, the hiker has the feeling he is not walking on earth
but instead treads some other
realm.

Takakkaw Falls in Yoho National Park, with a drop of 380 metres, is the third-highest falls in North America.

Mountain Goats are at home on the steepest slopes and wil jump distances as wide as three metres between ledges. When annoyed, they will stamp their forefeet or stick out their tongues.

This area above treeline in the Selkirk Range is grizzly country. As the dwarf willow turn to red in the fall, the great bear spends his days digging up the dens of the hoary marmot or the Columbia ground squirrel. Walking through this country, I always keep an extra watch, lest I too become a meal for the grizzly.

The Steller's Jay is a frequent
visitor to mountain camp-
sites. The white dot above his
eye marks him as an interior
subspecies.

Another camp-follower is the coyote. He can often be seen beside a mountain road begging for food from passing motorists. This particular fellow was caught trying to steal the author's lunch.

Situated on the eastern edge of the province, Mount Robson is the highest peak in the Canadian Rockies. So high that it creates its own weather, Mount Robson can simultaneously have a storm raging at its summit and the sun shining on its lower slopes.

Bill Brooks has been deeply involved with photographing the natural beauty of Canada and with the production of fine illustrated books since his graduation from the University of Toronto in 1962. His early experience was gained in the employ of several top Canadian photography and book publishing firms.

Casting a secure job aside, he went freelance in 1972 and set out on a journey of discovery, with the hope of finding both the real Canada and his place in it. Since then he has produced: *Canada in Colour, Ottawa: A Portrait of the Nation's Capital, The Mill, Wildlife of Canada, The Colour of Ontario, The Colour of Alberta, Seasons of Canada.* And now, *The Colour of British Columbia.*

Today, Bill Brooks' photographs of Canadian subjects are well-known, widely distributed, and frequently requested by major book, magazine, and advertising clients throughout the world . . . thereby allowing him the means in which to continue his journey of discovery.